MW00896306

Greater Than a Tourist Book Series Reviews from Readers

I think the series is wonderful and beneficial for tourists to get information before visiting the city.

-Seckin Zumbul, Izmir Turkey

I am a world traveler who has read many trip guides but this one really made a difference for me. I would call it a heartfelt creation of a local guide expert instead of just a guide.

-Susy, Isla Holbox, Mexico

New to the area like me, this is a must have!

-Joe, Bloomington, USA

This is a good series that gets down to it when looking for things to do at your destination without having to read a novel for just a few ideas.

-Rachel, Monterey, USA

Good information to have to plan my trip to this destination.

-Pennie Farrell, Mexico

Aptly titled, you won't just be a tourist after reading this book. You'll be greater than a tourist!

-Alan Warner, Grand Rapids, USA

Thank you for a fantastic book.

-Don, Philadelphia, USA

Lavina Solomonova

Great ideas for a port day.

-Mary Martin USA

Even though I only have three days to spend in San Miguel in an upcoming visit, I will use the author's suggestions to guide some of my time there. An easy read - with chapters named to guide me in directions I want to go.

-Robert Catapano, USA

Great insights from a local perspective! Useful information and a very good value!

-Sarah, USA

This series provides an in-depth experience through the eyes of a local. Reading these series will help you to travel the city in with confidence and it'll make your journey a unique one.

-Andrew Teoh, Ipoh, Malaysia

Tourists can get an amazing "insider scoop" about a lot of places from all over the world. While reading, you can feel how much love the writer put in it.

-Vanja Živković, Sremski Karlovci, Serbia

GREATER THAN A TOURIST – BROOKLYN NEW YORK USA

50 Travel Tips from a Local

Lavina Solomonova

Lavina Solomonova

Greater Than a Tourist- Brooklyn New York USA Copyright © 2017 by Lisa Rusczyk. All Rights Reserved.

All rights reserved. No part of this book may be reproduced in any form or by any electronic or mechanical means including information storage and retrieval systems, without permission in writing from the author. The only exception is by a reviewer, who may quote short excerpts in a review.

Cover Image: https://pixabay.com/en/waters-bridge-architecture-travel-3033752/
https://pixabay.com/en/marine-blue-sky-landscape-beach-3052592/

Greater Than a Tourist
Visit our website at www.GreaterThanaTourist.com

Lock Haven, PA
All rights reserved.

ISBN: 9781976946639

>TOURIST

50 TRAVEL TIPS FROM A LOCAL

Lavina Solomonova

BOOK DESCRIPTION

Are you excited about planning your next trip?
Do you want to try something new?
Would you like some guidance from a local?

If you answered yes to any of these questions, then this Greater Than a Tourist book is for you.

Greater Than a Tourist- Brooklyn New York by Lavina Solomonova offers the inside scoop on Brooklyn. Most travel books tell you how to travel like a tourist. Although there is nothing wrong with that, as part of the Greater Than a Tourist series, this book will give you travel tips from someone who has lived at your next travel destination.

In these pages you'll discover advice that will help you throughout your stay. This book will not tell you exact addresses or store hours but instead will give you excitement and knowledge from a local that you may not find in other smaller print travel books.

Travel like a local. Slow down, stay in one place, and get to know the people and the culture. By the time you finish this book, you will be eager and prepared to travel to your next destination.

Lavina Solomonova

TABLE OF CONTENTS

17. Little Skips
18. Bearcat Cafe
19. Uptown Roasters
20. Sweetleaf Coffee Roasters
21. Milk And Honey Cafe
22. Greene Grape Annex
23. Sweatshop
24. Variety Coffee Roasters
25. Freehold
26. Devocion
27. Budin
28. Bushwick Country Club
29. Battery Harris
30. Pig Beach
31. Lucky Dog
32. The Levee
33. Want Some Tacos?
34. Three Diamond Door
35. Forrest Point
36. Smorgasburg
37. Brooklyn Academy Of Music
38. Dekalb Market Hall
39. Baby's Alright
40. Peter Luger Steak House
41. Brooklyn Bowl
42. Sea
43. Nitehawk Cinema
44. Knitting Factory
Brooklyn

45. House of Yes
46. Union Hall
47. Brooklyn Bridge
48. make friends
49. keep on exploring
50. Carry an extra charger
TOP REASONS TO BOOK THIS TRIP
> TOURIST
GREATER THAN A TOURIST
> TOURIST
GREATER THAN A TOURIST

DEDICATION

This book is dedicated to Brooklyn.

Thank you for shaping me into the person I am today.

Lavina Solomonova

ABOUT THE AUTHOR

Lavina Solomonova is a writer and visual artist currently living in Brooklyn, New York. She is currently a student at John Jay College. She grew up in Russia, but has spend the past nine years living in Brooklyn.

Lavina Solomonova

HOW TO USE THIS BOOK

The Greater Than a Tourist book series was written by someone who has lived in an area for over three months. The goal of this book is to help travelers either dream or experience different locations by providing opinions from a local. The author has made suggestions based on their own experiences. Please do your own research before traveling to the area in case the suggested places are unavailable.

Lavina Solomonova

FROM THE PUBLISHER

Traveling can be one of the most important parts of a person's life. The anticipation and memories that you have are some of the best. As a publisher of the Greater Than a Tourist book series, as well as the popular 50 Things to Know book series, we strive to help you learn about new places, spark your imagination, and inspire you. Wherever you are and whatever you do I wish you safe, fun, and inspiring travel.

Lisa Rusczyk Ed. D.
CZYK Publishing

Lavina Solomonova

OUR STORY

Traveling is a passion of the "Greater than a Tourist" series creator. Lisa studied abroad in college, and for their honeymoon Lisa and her husband toured Europe. During her travels to Malta, an older man tried to give her some advice based on his own experience living on the island since he was a young boy. She was not sure if she should talk to the stranger but was interested in his advice. When traveling to some places she was wary to talk to locals because she was afraid that they weren't being genuine. Through her travels, Lisa learned how much locals had to share with tourists. Lisa created the "Greater Than a Tourist" book series to help connect people with locals. A topic that locals are very passionate about sharing.

Lavina Solomonova

WELCOME TO
> TOURIST

Lavina Solomonova

INTRODUCTION

I remember perfectly my first trip to New York, when I was on the bridge between Brooklyn and Manhattan, when I saw the skyscrapers. It was like an incredible dream.

-Diego Della Valle

Most of us have heard about Brooklyn, seen it on TV. One thing we should all keep in mind is that hearing about a place and experiencing it yourself are two totally different things. Whether you are traveling alone, with friends, family, or significant other, do not be afraid to take a step beyond your limits. There might be parts that you might dislike, and things you will fall in love with. Just accept it. In the end, you will learn more about yourself through exploring this diverse city. The tips provided in this book are just here to guide you, help you if you feel lost. I encourage you to explore Brooklyn beyond any tips anyone gives you.

Everyone has their own experience of Brooklyn, and so will you.

Lavina Solomonova

1. BEST TIME TO VISIT? ANYTIME!

Perhaps, it is what gives Brooklyn its charm—whether you visit it in the summer and spend your days under the burning sun on Coney Island, or freeze your toes skating in Prospect Park, Brooklyn is one of the few places you will not regret visiting during *any* time of the year.

Most of the things you would do in the summer, you can do in the winter. If you happen to come during the winter months, you will not be able to do things like sunbathing on the beach or letting the Luna Park lights fill you up with joy when the sun goes down. And if you plan your trip in the summer, you will miss out on feeling all that the cold months have to bring through the tips of your frozen toes on the ice-skating rink or while you get lost tale-like blocks of Dyker Heights. So, think about what is on the top of your bucket list and choose the season.

The in-between seasons—fall and spring—come with their own highlights. Early fall weather usually allows you to go to the beach and still get an eye-pleasing tan. If you want to sit on the bench of Prospect Park and watch the leaves change their color, then plan your trip sometime in November. If you visit the parks online site, you will find offers for Fall Foliage walks, Facts about Foliage, Fall Foliage Slideshow, and many other things every fall-lover. Depending on the weather, the ice rink opens at the end of October and is open all the way through March. For more information about hours, exact location and fees, visit their website for more. So, if you cannot make it out here during fall or winter, then come in spring! Visit Brooklyn Botanical garden for the magical walk through the cherry blossom.

Regardless of the season, after your visit, Brooklyn will find a place in your heart.

2. THE SUBWAY IS GOING TO BE YOUR BEST FRIEND

If you're familiar with the busy rhythm of NYC, then you should know that the Subway system is what, mainly, makes it work. The original subway tracks were designed to bring the working class from Brooklyn, Queens, and the Bronx to Manhattan. This is the reason for why sometimes it might seem hard to travel from one part of Brooklyn to another, for example getting to the south part of Brooklyn from the north and vise-versa. But it is not impossible! There might be times you will need to use the bus, but you can always Uber or use a bike. Rent a City Bike or find the closest bike rental.

If you do not have Google Maps on your phone, download it now! There are many apps out there for both ISO and Androids, and you might find some of them helpful. But Google Maps is easier to use and it always provides updated on delays and construction. It will provide with an alternate route when needed.

Also, if you do not have it yet, download Uber and set it up in advance! Uber Pools are a cheap and fast way to get around in Brooklyn, as well as anywhere else in the city.

Warning Art Lovers!

If you want to take a break from walking through the blocks filled with historic brownstones, stop by one of these soul-pleasing spaces. But before we proceed, it is advised for students to have their school ID at all times, since most, if not all, museums have student discounts.

Now, let's get started:

3. GO TO CLEARING

396 Johnson Ave
Brooklyn, NY 11206

This is a Brooklyn branch of a gallery in Brussels, Belgium, located in Bushwick. Its focus in the young artists who produce up-to-date art in response to the modern world. The admission is FREE! Go to their site for more information. Get there by taking the L to Morgan Av, or J/M/Z to Flushing Avenue. Stop by Roberta's for a bite of freshly baked, brick-oven pizza.

4. BROOKLYN MUSEUM

200 Eastern Pkwy
Brooklyn, NY 11238

Located on the edge of the Prospect Park, Brooklyn Museum is the third largest museum in New York City and holds over a million exhibits. The work always changes, so be sure to check out their site for what is being displayed now, as well as the exact address, hours of operation and admission. It is a few minutes' walk from Park Slope, and if you are not in the area hop on the 2 or 3 train to the Eastern Parkway Brooklyn Museum Station. If those two trains are not available to you, take the S train to the Botanic Garden stop, 4/5 to Franklin Avenue, B/Q to 7th Avenue—there are lots of ways!

Brooklyn Museum offers free admission on the first Saturday of every month.

5. ARTS IN GENERAL

145 Plymouth St
Brooklyn, NY 11201

This is a smaller, non-profit, contemporary art space. The gallery displays a wide range of art, through which the artists speak to today's world. And it is FREE. Art in General is located in the heart of DUMBO. So, while you are in the area, enjoying the view of the bridges, head down to 145 Plymouth St or get there via train, by taking the F to York Street, A/C to High Street, or 2/3 to Clark Street. For more information about the gallery check for their website online. You can head over to, one of DUMBO's most chic restaurants, Atrium Dumbo where you can art-talk over a drink and one of their many delicious plates.

Lavina Solomonova

6. THE NEW YORK TRANSIT MUSUEM

Boerum Pl & Schermerhorn St
Brooklyn, NY 11201

If you are going to be using the train to explore Brooklyn, might as well make a stop by the New York Transit Museum to learn a little (or a lot) more about the history of New York's subway, bus, bridge, commuter rail and tunnel system. If you are already in Brooklyn Heights, then make your way to the intersection of Schermerhorn St and Boerum Pl. You can also take the 4/5 to Borough Hall, F to Jay St-Metro Tech, A/C/G to Hoyt-Schermerhorn, or B/D/N/Q/R/W to DeKalb Avenue. If you are looking to grab a bite before or after the museum visit, head to DeKalb Market Hall, where you will find over 40 famous New York Vendors, all in one space! Talk about being at a right place at a right time.

7. DID SOMEONE SAY ART!?

Want to turn this visit into a gallery-hopping? Check out the following art spaces in the area and explore all different areas/styles of art that Brooklyn and its people has to offer.:

SIGNAL
260 Johnson Ave

Luhring Augustine
25 Knickerbocker Ave

ArtHelix
289 Meserole St

Microscope Gallery
1329 Willoughby Avenue

Theodore:Art
56 Bogart St

The Parlour
791 Bushwick Ave

SARDINE
286 Stanhope St

Storefront Ten Eyck
324 Ten Eyck St

Kid-Time

As much as you can go bar-hopping, through the hip bars of Brooklyn, you can spend a day dedicated to your child or younger sibling. The following list is mainly focused on the entertainment of the little ones, some of them are all-age friendly. If you do not have kids to bring keep on reading anyway, because most of the listed places are worth visiting on your own.

21

8. VISIT LEFRAK CENTER AT LAKESIDE

171 East Dr
Brooklyn, NY 11225

You can either ice skate or roller skate here, depending on the season. The roller skating rink opens in the end of May until late October, so if you are visiting during this time grab your roller skates and make your way to the LeFrank Center at Lakeside of Prospect Park. If you don't have anything to bring, you can rent the skates for $6 on a weekday and $7 on a weekend. The rental for ice skates is similar. The ice skating rink opens at the end of October and remains open up until April. Visit their site for more information and other activities by the lake of Prospect Park. You can get here by taking the Q to Parkside Ave, B/S to Prospect Park Subway Station, 5 to Winthrop Street or F/G to Fort Hamilton Pkwy. If you get hungry, you do not need to wander too far off since *Bluestone Cafe*, located in the same building, offers a variety of health-conscious sandwiches, sides and drink, or wander outside of the park and make your way to the *Blessings Café*, where you will find a wide range of breakfast and comfort-food dishes.

9. GO SEE THE PROSPECT PARK ZOO

450 Flatbush Ave
Brooklyn, NY 11225

Want to continue your day in the same relaxing manner? You do not have to go far. Walk up to the spacious zoo located in the Prospect Park. The zoo holds over 100 different species. A perfect spot to take your kid, or just come here on your own. Who does not love animals? Visit their site to get your ticker, view the schedule or look for answers to the questions you may have. You can get here by taking the B/Q/S to Prospect Park Subway Station, 4/5 to Franklin Ave, or, if you would like to take a long walk across the park, F/G to 7th Ave. Afterward, walk over to *Bluebird* on 504 Flatbush Ave, and enjoy a drink, and a snack for your kid, on a patio. It is also dog-friendly.

10. ROLLER SKATING WITH A VIEW

150 Furman St, Pier 2
Brooklyn, NY 11201

Another roller skating rink, but this time with a view! Enjoy the waterfront rink the post-card view of Manhattan and the bridges. Not in the mood to roller skate? The pier also provides spaces for basketball, handball, shuffleboard and bocce ball courts. Get here by taking the N/R/W to Court St, A/c to High Street-Brooklyn Bridge, or 2/3 to Clark Street Station. Stay refreshed with the fresh juices from *Lizzmonade*. If you are looking to grab a bite head over to *Jack the Horse Tavern* on 66 Hicks St or to *Iron Chef House* on 92 Clark St for delicious Japanese dishes.

11. AN ADRENALINE RUSH

99 Plymouth St
Brooklyn, NY 11201

DUMBO Boulders is an outdoor rock-climbing area, in the heart of Brooklyn. Join your child for a climbing session right under the bridge. Due to the weather, there is no admission in the winter. Visit their website for scheduling and other information. Get here by taking the F to York Street Subway, or A/C to High Street Brooklyn Bridge. Walk over to the famous Juliana's for a freshly baked pizza pie

12. RECESS DUMBO

81 Washington St
Brooklyn, NY 11201

Your child still has energy after that rock-climbing? Then head over to Recess Dumbo which offers play-space, a variety of classes and birthday parties. You can even leave your child to play and make new friends, while you go for lunch. Get here by taking the F to York Street Subway, or A/C to High Street Brooklyn Bridge. While your little one is enjoying the play-time, walk down to Bluestone Lane, 55 Prospect St, for a cup of fresh coffee.

13. DIVE INTO THE OCEAN, IN THE CITY

602 Surf Ave
Brooklyn, NY 11224

The New York Aquarium is located on the boardwalk of Coney Island, this is the oldest continually operating aquarium in the United States. Explore the sea creatures with your child, and check out their site for special events and ticket offers. Get there by taking the F/Q to W 8 St-NY Aquarium, or D/N to Coney Island-Stillwell Av. Take a walk on the boardwalk afterward, and, if the weather allows, go for a swim on the beach!

14. HAVE A BLAST AT THE LUNA PARK

1000 Surf Ave
Brooklyn, NY 11224

New York City's famous amusement park is located in Coney Island. It's got rides for both kids and adult, along with different snacks and drinks vendors. The park is closed during the winter, but it opens at the end of March and remains open until the middle of fall. Feel the adrenaline rushing through every inch of your body while you ride the historical Cyclone. Get there by taking D/F/Q/N to Coney Island-Stillwell Av. Don't forget to grab a hot-dog at *Nathan's Famous*, on 1310 Surf Ave, and stop by *Coney Art Walls*, on 3050 Stillwell Ave, to check out the beautiful graffiti walls. Take a walk on the boardwalk, enjoy the variety of different food stands and fireworks on a Friday night.

15. TWINKLE PLAYSPACE

144 Frost St
Brooklyn, NY 11211

Located in Williamsburg, Twinkle Playspace is a children's amusement center. Come here with your child for a birthday party or just for an indoor play-space that every kid will love. Get here by taking the L to Graham Ave, or G to Metropolitan Ave. Afterwards, stop by the famous Bagel Store on 754 Metropolitan Ave for your fix of the rainbow bagel. Do not forget to pair it with one of many delicious fillings. Get funky with it!

Lavina Solomonova

16. BROOKLYN BOTANIC GARDENS

990 Washington Ave
Brooklyn, NY 11225

Brooklyn's 52-acre garden is located in Prospect Park. You can visit it during any time of the year. The garden has many unique parts, like Japanese Garden. If you are visiting in the spring, make sure to attend the Cherry Blossom Festival. Get there by taking the S to Botanic Garden Stop, 2/3/4/5 to Franklin Ave, or B/Q to Prospect Park. If you get hungry and do not want to leave the park just yet, head over to *Yellow Magnolia Café.*

...Coffee Time

If you think of a New Yorker, you probably imagine a person in a strict suite, in a rush, with a cup of coffee in hand. Well, this image is partially correct. Brooklyn's coffee culture is slightly different from Manhattan's. While you might see people running around with a morning coffee in hand, in Brooklyn you will find cozy coffee shops filled with people. Some of them are so full at times you will not be able to find a table. But do not let that discourage you! This just shows how coffee-culture in Brooklyn has grown and changed over the past few years. You will often find people chatting over a cup of latte for hours, doing their work, or just relaxing with a book in hand. There are tons of coffee shops in Brooklyn, but I'm going to list few of the best ones. The following coffee shops are perfect for any occasion:

17. LITTLE SKIPS

941 Willoughby Ave
Brooklyn, NY 11221

This hip coffee shop is known to be one of the best coffee shops in Bushwick. In addition to their freshly brewed coffee, they offer a variety of delicious sandwiches and a selection of vegan and gluten-free options. There are people always coming in and out, and it might seem busy at times, but peek in and chances are you will be able to find yourself a table. Since the weekend tends to get busy, they usually turn off their Wi-Fi. So, leave your work for later, and philosophize over a cup of coffee. If you stick around until the evening, you might come across an art show or some live music. Get here by taking the J/M/Z to Myrtle Ave, G to Myrtle-Willoughby Ave, or L to DeKalb Ave.

18. BEARCAT CAFE

150 Manhattan Ave
Brooklyn, NY 11206

Coffee shop in the daytime, bar in the evening—what else can you ask for? This Café is perfect to get a sandwich or just to come and get some work done. The egg-croissant sandwich will have you coming back one too many times. Get here by taking the L to Montrose Ave, J/M/Z to Lorimer Street Station, or G to Metropolitan Ave.

19. UPTOWN ROASTERS

355 7th Ave
Brooklyn, NY 11215

This coffee shop takes its name from the original uptown location, but this Park Slope location will provide you with quality coffee and enough seating area. Unlike the previous two coffee shop, this one does not provide a wide range of sandwiches. Instead, they have fresh pastries to accompany your cup of coffee. Get here by taking the F/G to 7 Ave, or D/N/R/W to 9 St. Make sure to walk around the neighborhood to see all the historical brownstones.

20. SWEETLEAF COFFEE ROASTERS

159 Freeman St
Brooklyn, NY 11222

Unlike its other locations in Manhattan, this spacious coffee shops offers a large, cozy space, with comfortable sofas. When it starts to get warmer out, they open their garage doors, to allow more fresh air some into the room while you are working on your computer, or just enjoying a cup of cappuccino with the chatter-noise in the background. Outdoor seating is also available, if the weather allows it. Get here by the G train to Nassau Ave.

21. MILK AND HONEY CAFE

1119 Newkirk Ave
Brooklyn, NY 11230

This café, located in the West Midwood, offers a wide range of egg plates, salads, sandwiches and comfort food. This is a perfect place to get breakfast or brunch and get work done. It gets busy on the weekend, so they do not allow any laptops on the tables. When it gets warmer outside, they open their garage-like doors and provide outdoor seating. Get here by taking the Q/B to Newkrik Plaza or F to 18 Avenue Station.

22. GREENE GRAPE ANNEX

753 Fulton St
Brooklyn, NY 11217

This is a café/bar, not the Greene Grape is a grocery/wine store in Fort Greene—it is easy to make a mistake sometimes, especially when the names are so similar. Alongside with their coffee, they offer pastries and sandwiches. They have lots of space, so you are most likely to bump into freelancers working on their laptops. Get there by taking the A/C to Lafayette Ave, B/D/N/Q/R/W to DeKalb Ave, or 4/5 to Bergen Ave.

23. SWEATSHOP

232 Metropolitan Ave
Brooklyn, NY 11211

This hip coffee shop is located in the heart of Williamsburg. So, if you are looking for a place to relax after a long day of shopping, this is the spot. The Australian designers who opened this place made sure to provide their costumers with an eye-pleasing décor, cozy atmosphere and an outdoor seating for spring, summer, and fall. Get here by taking L to Bedford Ave, or G to Metropolitan Ave.

24. VARIETY COFFEE ROASTERS

146 Wyckoff Ave
Brooklyn, NY 11237

Another cozy Bushwick coffee shop that offers fresh coffee and pastries. You can be sure that you will find a seat here if you are looking to chat over a cup of tea or coffee. Get here by taking the L to DeKalb Ave, or M to Seneca Ave.

25. FREEHOLD

45 S 3rd St
Brooklyn, NY 11249

Looking for a coffee shop with comfortable chairs to spend your hours away? Freehold is the answer. Located by the Williamsburg Bridge, this coffee shop provides spacious outdoor and indoor seating. In the evening, this space turns into a bar. On a weekend you might even come across a party. Get here by taking the J/M/Z to Marcy Ave, or G to Metropolitan Ave.

26. DEVOCION

69 Grand St
Brooklyn, NY 11249

Few blocks away from the coffee shop above, Devoción offers a space with couches and tables. Stop by and feel what they mean when they say industrial Brooklyn Style. The exposed brick walls, a skylight, and repurposed pipes will inspire you to change some things around in your own apartment. Plus, they roast their own coffee! Get here by taking the J/M/Z to Marcy Ave, or G to Metropolitan Ave.

27. BUDIN

114 Greenpoint Ave
Brooklyn, NY 11222

This coffee shop is located in Greenpoint. It is a little bit different from what has been listed before, since other than just a coffee shop or a café-in-the-daytime & bar-in-the-evening kind of thing, this is not just a coffee shop but also a boutique. So, you can sip on your coffee and shop all the same time! Get here by taking the G to Nassau Ave.

Dog-Friendly Restaurants and Bars

Wondering whether to bring your dog with you? Brooklyn says, DO IT! The following bars and restaurants are perfect for spending some time with your dog. And even if you do not have one, they are worth the try:

28. BUSHWICK COUNTRY CLUB

618 Grand St
Brooklyn, NY 11211

Unlike other country clubs, this one is not expensive and does not have a dress code. If you are in the East Williamsburg, stop by to enjoy happy hour cocktails and bar games and mini golf. Most importantly, you can do that with your dog by your side! Get here by taking the G to Metropolitan Ave, or L to Graham Ave.

29. BATTERY HARRIS

64 Frost St
Brooklyn, NY 11211

Enjoy Caribbean Dished and their hip décor, while you sip on a frozen Dark N Stormy! They offer both indoor and outdoor seating. Their cute atmosphere will not allow you to stop sending pictures to your friends or sharing your meal on Instagram. If you are bringing your dog, make sure to walk over to McCarren Park and let him run loose in the dog's park. Get here by taking the L to Bedford Ave, or the G to Metropolitan Ave.

Lavina Solomonova

30. PIG BEACH

480 Union St
Brooklyn, NY 11231

Whether you are trying to catch up with an old friend or getting together with the family, this is a perfect place to come. Their BBQ and a wide range of beers will defiantly have you coming back. They also provide outdoor bar games. Get here by taking the F/G to Carroll Street, or D/N/R/W to Union St.

31. LUCKY DOG

303 Bedford Ave
Brooklyn, NY 11211

Want to dedicate some time to your dog, but also want to have some drinks? Lucky Dog is the place you should be heading over to. Majority of their costumers do not come in this bar without their dogs. They have a backyard, where you can let your dog run around and make friends, and, perhaps, make some friends yourself over a glass of beer. Since this bar's focus is the dog-friendly policy, they do not serve any food, but they do allow you to bring your own food or order it for delivery. If you do not feel like doing that, do not stress it. It is located in the heart of Williamsburg, so there are many other places you can go to for a bite. Get here by taking the L to Bedford Ave, G to Metropolitan Ave, or J/M/Z to Marcy Ave.

32. THE LEVEE

212 Berry St
Brooklyn, NY 11211

Come here for a beer, booze, snacks, and play some board games, darts, and pool. In addition to that all, bring your pup! This is one of the few hip and cheap places located in Williamsburg. Get here by taking the L to Bedford Ave, G to Metropolitan Ave, or J/M/Z to Marcy Ave.

33. WANT SOME TACOS?

225 Wythe Ave
Brooklyn, NY 11230

Cafe de la Esquina is a hip, retro, Mexican diner and is located in Williamsburg, providing an outdoor patio. Cafe de la Esquina made Puppy Brunch possible! If you do not have a dog to bring, you will still enjoy their authentically-made Mexican dishes. Get here by taking the L to Bedford Ave, G to Metropolitan Ave, or J/M/Z to Marcy Ave.

Lavina Solomonova

34. THREE DIAMOND DOOR

211 Knickerbocker Ave
Brooklyn, NY 11237

Whether you come here with your pup or not, this bar should be on your list to visit. Located in Bushwick, this bar's chic décor and on-tap prosecco will make you feel like the time machine does exist, and you have traveled a few decades back in time. Get here by taking the L to Jefferson St.

35. FORREST POINT

970 Flushing Ave
Brooklyn, NY 11206

Bushwick cannot stop surprising the Brooklynites with its hip restaurants. Stop by Forrest Point for delicious Mediterranean dishes and inventive cocktails. They provide both outdoor and indoor sitting, and, most importantly, amazing service. Get here by taking the J/M/Z to Flushing Ave, or L to Montrose Ave.

Highlights of Brooklyn

Go to any of these places with friends, or family or on a date!

36. SMORGASBURG

90 Kent Ave
Brooklyn, NY 11211
    &*
Prospect Park, Well House Dr
Brooklyn, NY 11225

Warm weather brings opens up lots of things that get closed for the winter season, and one of the is Smorgasburg. Every Brooklynite looks forward these open spaces to get occupied with over 70 different vendors who serve the most popular New York City Food. The location in Williamsburg is open every Saturday, and Prospect park location is open on Sundays. Check out their website for the exact schedule, since it may vary. To get to the Williamsburg location, take the L to Bedford Ave, and to get to the Prospect Park location, take the B/Q/S to Prospect Park.

Lavina Solomonova

37. BROOKLYN ACADEMY OF MUSIC

30 Lafayette Ave
Brooklyn, NY 11217

Brooklyn Academy of Music, also referred to as BAM, is known as New York's multi-art center of avant-garde performances. This is one Brooklyn's famous and most visited places. Check out their website to see what amazing shows they have to offer while you are here. Get here by taking the B/D/N/Q/R/W to Atlantic Ave- Barclay Center, A/C to Lafayette Ave, or 4/5 to Nevins Ave.

38. DEKALB MARKET HALL

445 Albee Square W
Brooklyn, NY 11201

Another space filled with food! This time, it is open all year long, and unlike Smorgasburg, there will not be any long lines. The space provided over 40 vendors from all over New York City, showcasing the city's cultural diversity. If you did not make it on time for Smorgasburg, DeKlab Market Hall will offer some of the same vendors you would see at Smorgasburg. Get here by taking the B/N/Q/R/W to DeKalb Ave, 4/5 to Nevins St, or A/C/G to Hoyt-Schermerhorn.

39. BABY'S ALRIGHT

146 Broadway
Brooklyn, NY 11211

This venue is separated into three parts—dining, bar and live music, bar, and a dance floor. What makes it even more special is that you can walk through all three the whole nights. You can check out their calendar on their website to see what special events and live bands they got for tonight. Come here on a weekend for creative drinks and brunch. Get here by taking the J/M/Z to Marcy Ave.

40. PETER LUGER STEAK HOUSE

178 Broadway
Brooklyn, NY 11211

Brooklyn's famous steakhouse is located in Williamsburg, steps away from *Baby's All Right*! They serve delicious, aged beef with a variety of side dishes. The old-school décor will make you feel like you are in a German beer hall. Make sure to bring cash, since it's a cash-only restaurant. It is advices to give them a call-in advance a make a reservation since they are always busy. This should tell you a lot already! Get here by taking the J/M/Z to Marcy Ave.

41. BROOKLYN BOWL

61 Wythe Ave
Brooklyn, NY 11249

This is more than your regular bowling alley. It's low-light environment, high-tech lanes, and hip décor makes it a great place to get together with your friends to play some bowling, sip on some drinks and enjoy the food provided by Blue Ribbon. The cheery-on-the-top is their stage, where they hold live music shows and a dance floor. It cannot get any better! Check out their website to see the bands that are going to be playing while you are visiting. Get here by taking the L to Bedford Ave, or G to Nassau Ave.

42. SEA

114 N 6th St
Brooklyn, NY 11249

Located just a few blocks away from Brooklyn Bowl is this Thai restaurant with a pond in the middle of it and fleshy décor. This is one of the best and relatively cheap Thai restaurants in Brooklyn. They have a large variety of food and drinks. It gets busy in the evening. So, if you do not want to wait for too long, give them a call and make your reservation. Get there by taking the L to Bedford Ave, or G to Nassau Ave.

43. NITEHAWK CINEMA

136 Metropolitan Ave
Brooklyn, NY 11249

This is a small movie theater, which, instead of popcorn, serves good and drinks while you enjoy the movie. The rooms are smaller than a general movie theater provides, so make sure you check out their website and get your tickets in advance. They screen some of the most unique movies. Get there by taking the L to Bedford Ave, or G to Nassau Ave.

44. KNITTING FACTORY BROOKLYN

361 Metropolitan Ave,
Brooklyn, NY 11211

Do not get fooled by the name! This is just another spacious Williamsburg venue for live music. They also serve food, but it is good to keep in mind that this is an adult-only restaurant. Check their website to see what bands are performing soon and get your tickets! Get here by taking the J/M/Z to Marcy Ave, L to Bedford Ave, or G to Nassau Ave

45. HOUSE OF YES

2 Wyckoff Ave
Brooklyn, NY 11237

Visit House of Yes on any night of the week and you will start to understand what they mean when they say, "New York never sleeps". This funky venue provides a variety of different events throughout the week, showcasing circus, dance cabaret and other performances. For most of the night you will be asked to get a ticket. Although you might be able to get a ticket at the door, it is better to get in advance from their website. Get there by taking the L to Jefferson St.

46. UNION HALL

702 Union St
Brooklyn, NY 11215

Located in Park Slope, this is an event venue where you can come and enjoy a drink with the library-like décor. Stick around until the evening and catch a live performance. Check out their calendar on their website to see which nights are karaoke nights and sing your soul out. They also have stand up comedy shows. So, choose wisely! Get here by taking the B/Q to 7 Ave, 4/5 to Grand Army Plaza, or D/N/R/W to Union St.

47. BROOKLYN BRIDGE

It might seem a little bit confusing when it comes to figuring out how to walk up to the Brooklyn Bridge, but do not get discouraged! First, grab yourself a cone of freshly made ice-cream at *Brooklyn Ice Cream Factory,* on 1 Water St, and then head over to the intersection of Tillary Street and Boerum Place. That's where you will be able to access the bridge. Get here by taking the A/C to Hight Street-Brooklyn Bridge, or F to York Street. Enjoy your walk through the historical bridge!

48. MAKE FRIENDS

This might seem like a strange tip, but do not be afraid to go out there and make new friends. Some might say New Yorkers are rude. Some of them could be at times, but that does not mean all of them are. If you are sitting in a coffee shop alone, you might hear a stranger sitting next to you or the barista comment on your look or the weather. Entertain it! You never know what new connections and friendships you might make.

49. KEEP ON EXPLORING

There are so many more place that did not make the tip-list of this guide. As you walk through the blocks of Brooklyn, do not be afraid to get lost. Go into each place that looks interesting to you. Just like New York City as a whole, Brooklyn contains a great cultural diversity which reflects in the restaurants, cafes, bars, art galleries, and even the streets themselves. Carry a camera with you at all times! Or just make sure your phone is charged because you will want to capture every moment.

50. CARRY AN EXTRA CHARGER

Perhaps, this tip might seem silly and obvious, but just wanted to remind you to always carry a carry-on charger with you as well as an extra charger that you can plug your phone into at a coffee shop. You will be surprised how fast your phone will go out of battery by using the maps and the camera.

TOP REASONS TO BOOK THIS TRIP

Food: Brooklyn offers tons of restaurants and cafes, where you will be able to taste the diversity of the city

Coffee Culture: Brooklyn's growing coffee culture has opened doors to many independent coffee shops   through which the coffee has turned into a form of art.

Art: you will find art everywhere you go. Just keep your eyes open.

Lavina Solomonova

> TOURIST
GREATER THAN A TOURIST

Visit GreaterThanATourist.com:
http://GreaterThanATourist.com

Sign up for the Greater Than a Tourist Newsletter:
http://eepurl.com/cxspyf

Follow us on Facebook:
https://www.facebook.com/GreaterThanATourist

Follow us on Pinterest:
http://pinterest.com/GreaterThanATourist

Follow us on Instagram:
http://Instagram.com/GreaterThanATourist

Lavina Solomonova

> TOURIST
GREATER THAN A TOURIST

Please leave your honest review of this book on Amazon and Goodreads. Thank you. We appreciate your positive and constructive feedback. Thank you.

Lavina Solomonova

Made in United States
North Haven, CT
22 April 2022

18466484R00039